AF586518

UNIVERSITY
OF
JOHANNESBURG

Poison

A Play in One Act

Sandile Mdlongwa

UJ Press

Poison: A Play in One Act

Published by UJ Press
University of Johannesburg
Library
Auckland Park Kingsway Campus
PO Box 524
Auckland Park
2006
https://ujonlinepress.uj.ac.za/

Compilation © Sandile Mdlongwa 2023
Chapters © Sandile Mdlongwa 2023
Images © Sandile Mdlongwa 2023
Published Edition © Sandile Mdlongwa 2023

First published 2023

https://doi.org/10.36615/9781776424290

978-1-77642-256-0-0 (Paperback)
978-1-77642-242-9-0 (PDF)
978-1-77642-256-1-7 (EPUB)
978-1-77642-256-2-4 (XML)

This publication had been submitted to a rigorous double-blind peer-review process prior to publication and all recommendations by the reviewers were considered and implemented before publication.

Language Editor: Louis Botes
Cover design: Hester Roets, UJ Graphic Design Studio
Typeset in 10/13pt Merriweather Light

Contents

For my mother and guardian angel.

Patience Mafungwase Mdlongwa (1972–1998)

In Memoriam

Until we meet again in the next life.

'I was holding back my tears man; since I relate to the story so much, emotional yet informative and educational. Looking forward to more of them. A few hours I was able to forget about my situation and learn and yes I learnt . . . a lot. If only those who didn't see Poison knew what they missed.'
– **Regomoditswe Tshepang Thebe**

'Very educational and relates to the reality we live in. Well written, portrayed and executed.' – **Katlego Mokgau**

'It was beautiful, very informative. The charisma of [the] actors is wonderful. The message is very clear and lucid.'
– **Ntombizanele Mncube** *(librarian)*

'Challenges the mind and questions society.'– **Nhlanhla Nhlapo**

'The play Poison was very educational in the sense that it seeks to address the past and current misconceptions of men's attitudes towards the changing roles of women in society. In my observation, the play empowers both men and women.' – **Ermonia Manhique**

'The play is crafted in glitz and humor. There were times I laughed and there were times I was broken. Such creativity made the play more interesting, despite its core educational background.' – **Makwandiswe Sithole**

'The actors and actresses' performances were great. I was intrigued by the context of the story. We live in a society where men have more privileges than women. The concept was well executed, both informative and practical. I am very proud of Sandile Mdlongwa for coming up with a concept that many people are not ready to talk about.'
– **Patient Smangele Nhlapo**

'It could spark a robust debate across the country.'
– **Mpho Xabadi**

Poison: A Play in One Act

'The play was a bang. I could not stop thinking about it. Poison is very educational, powerful, eye-opening and informative. I've learnt a lot from it. I enjoyed the play so much and hated it to see it end.'
– **Itumeleng Hope Mothlabe**

'Very motivating for us as youths to get involved and stop with the ignorance. I see the play sending a huge message to communities and the world.' – **Xavi Tivane**

'I find the play Poison very enlightening and interesting. It feeds the brain with knowledge.' - **John Ndaba**

'I enjoyed the show and I have learnt that all human beings are equal and we should be treated the same.'
– **Alice Ndaba**

'The play is very educational and informative.'
– **Vusi Matshila**

About the Author

Sandile Mdlongwa is a results-oriented and self-driven person offering well-developed critical thinking, analytical skills and the crucial ability to solve complex problems. He holds two degrees; a BA in Politics and a post-graduate BA Honours in Politics and International Relations. These degrees were obtained at the University of Johannesburg (UJ). In 2015, Mr Mdlongwa was placed on the Dean's list – the list of top achievers – at the UJ Faculty of Humanities. Mr Mdlongwa has a certificate from Harvard University on Rhetoric: The Art of Persuasive Writing and Public Speaking.

In 2017, at the tender age of 23, Sandile published a book titled; *The Staff of Legends: Fees Must Fall.* His book captured the perspectives of students during the 'Fees Must Fall' movement and sparked critical debate across universities and wider society. This signified a critical moment for Sandile as a promising young academic and demonstrated his remarkable writing ability and research skills.

In 2021, an article on the website *Briefly South African News* described Sandile Mdlongwa as *'a beacon of hope.'*

Preface

The play *Poison* premiered on Tuesday, 8 November 2022 at the Soweto Theatre, Johannesburg, South Africa. The play ran for three days in the Blue Theatre – Soweto Theatre's second largest theatre, which has a capacity of 120 seats.

Despite being performed during the week (from Tuesday until Thursday), the show managed to attract an audience of more than 250 people.

Poison is a one-act play with three scenes and five cast members. Noteworthy, its protagonist is a female.

The play falls under the genre of 'protest theatre'. Protest theatre is a form of political theatre that uses performance to raise awareness of social and political issues. Performers in protest theatre aim to provoke change or raise awareness by challenging the status quo. Noteworthy, protest theatre encourages people to get involved in any cause that will advance humanity, for example, fighting for environmental protection or peace.

In the context of South Africa, protest theatre rose to prevalence in response to the apartheid laws. South African playwrights such as Athol Fugard, Mbongeni Ngema, John Kani and many others produced plays that criticised the apartheid laws. These plays also encouraged people to get involved in the struggle against the apartheid regime. As an example, in the 1970s, the play *Woza Albert*, a collaborative effort between Percy Mtwa and Mbongeni Ngema, became an important form of expression for those who were suffering and oppressed by the apartheid regime.

On the other hand, the play *Poison* falls under the genre of 'protest theatre' as a theatre of testimony, defiance and determination. Mdlongwa used this play as a vehicle to explore the factors that contribute to the problem of gender-based violence and femicide. These issues involve patriarchy, toxic femininity, toxic masculinity, stereotypes, conservative views, poverty, alcohol and drug abuse. This play aims to re-educate society and it uses powerful rhetorical tools (logos, ethos and pathos) to persuade its audience.

Introduction

Matsobane Ledwaba

The definition and meaning of Gender-Based-Violence (GBV) varies according to people's perspectives and origins. Others are of the view that GBV is solely about the physical and emotional abuse of women, the Lesbian, Gay, Bisexual, Transgender, Queer and Intersex Community (LGBTQI) and other vulnerable groups. Others are of the view that GBV and the legality around it is nothing but a weapon formed against men. However, the acronym GBV refers to any type of harm that is perpetrated against a person or group of people because of their factual or perceived sex, gender, sexual orientation and/or gender identity. However, it must be taken into consideration that it is mostly women, children, the LGBTQI Community and other vulnerable groups who fall prey to the scourge of GBV.

Nonetheless, educating communities about the problem of GBV is a difficult task. It needs an above class room set up. This is the case because people in general, as noted above; have differing views and positions. These views and positions are affected by one's culture, religion, beliefs, gender, origin and environment.

The play Poison seeks to address the issues of gender-politics objectively. Mdlongwa uses logic and the element of pathos in order to appeal to our emotions. This is an effective tool because a lot of people can relate. Well, the reality is, all of us as human beings have one or two emotional experiences that are relatable in a broader perspective.

In addition, the logic of Poison seeks to provoke a debate in society, to challenge the mind to think, to promote a healthy engagement and to advocate for a change. The lingo and content of the play Poison is raw, uncompromising and original. It is like a fresh uncut diamond, very high in value. On the other hand, the play Poison exonerates the writer.

Foreword

Sello Maake Ka-Ncube

Sandile Mdlongwa aptly describes Poison as a play falling under protest theatre. This is a theatre piece with an unequivocal intention to be provocative. A tool for social advocacy and will engender change in the process.

One of the definition of Poison according to Merriam-Webster is: A substance that through its chemical action usually kills, injures, or impairs an organism. Something destructive or harmful. In muted tones we have witnessed how poisonous masculinity and the equally poisonous femininity creates a subject that we are "now" very uncomfortable to engage in. Through one of his characters in the play, Sandile cudgels our brains when he says: "Please learn to disagree with each other without being violently disagreeable. Agree to a point out of conviction and persuasion. Do not disagree out of spite. Let ideas and evidence debate, do not debate each other out of emotions and feelings."

He puts five characters around a table to deliberate a weighty issue on Gender Based Violence and Femicide. The prevalence of this scourge during the covid 19 pandemic, was dubbed the shadow pandemic. This even prompted a march to the Union Building in the midst of the pandemic.

One can ask the question, why do we have high rates of Gender Base Violence and Femicide? One of the answers I came up with from my observation is that we learned the language of violence, often by precept from our conquerors. The history of South Africa from the inception of colonialism has been that of "skop, skiet and donner." Loosely translated in English, it means; 'kick, shoot and strike. Land dispossession and the migrant labour system made an ass of African people social order. Men were separated from their households and forced into same sex compound. Women left alone to run households. Children growing without there fathers.

It is common cause that every child needs to be raised by both parents. However, that was not to be in African communities. Understanding, and its corollary, harmonious relationships, was to be a very scarce commodity in couples living in urban areas as people were uprooted from their well established social constructs of their habitats into new constructs of the dog eat dog worlds. Survivals of the most brutal. Humaneness, the spirit of 'Ubuntu', the very source of good neighbourliness, not as proposed by the father of Apartheid , H.F. Verwoerd, was cast into the wind.

At its heart 'Poison' pleads for constructive engagement. Advocates for a surgical interrogation of how we take up these causes against GBV+F. Are we taking them up as means of sustenance or truly want to see the back of the scourge? And if that is case, what and how are we doing that?There is a saying: "Iva likhishwa ngelinye iva. Loosely translated this saying means to remove a thorn, you use another thorn. For us to truly deal with this scourge we truly need to pit truth against truth. Sandile's characters guides us in this regard. To truly cut to the chase, we need to acknowledge our propensities of fallibility and start with introspection and observe the tendencies of the mind, and then closely examine them. In process embark on a stern but unmistaken self analysis which would lead to self adjustment. In the process stop ourselves from being slaves to our impulses but masters of that we survey.

Truth and Spin doctoring like water and paraffin albeit bearing same colour, don't mix. We require an unequivocal bias to the true cause of GBV+F, as Sandile's one-act play informs.

Poison

A Play in One Act

Sandile Mdlongwa

Cast of Characters

Edward:	A member of the Cultural and Traditional Committee
Nelson:	A master's student at the University of Comfivaba
Michael:	A member of the One Africa Movement
Itumeleng:	A member of the Township Domestic Affairs Movement
Buhlebendalo:	National chairperson of the Women's Front Unit

Act 1

Scene 1

SETTING: A huge rectangular table is placed in the middle of the conference room. Around the table are five chairs. Two chairs are placed on one the length of the table and two chairs on the other length, directly opposite to each other. On one side of the table's width is a chair facing the audience. A glass of water, a pen and a notebook are placed in order from left to right in front of each of the chairs. A big jar of water stands in the middle of the table.

AT RISE: Five delegates enter the conference room procedurally, one after the other. They are all well-dressed, and they all look stunning.

'Rhetoric, logic and fallacies'

EDWARD

(He positions himself on his chair comfortably.)

(He lifts and adjusts the frame of his eyeglasses, clears his throat, and coughs a little bit.)

(He glances over the table one more time and begins to speak).

(*with a stern expression*) Good morning ladies and gentlemen.

If you are part of the LGBTQI community, and you are present in this session, consider yourself greeted as well (*with a smile on his face*). *We mustn't leave* anyone behind.

Nonetheless, before I speak any further, I humbly request that each of you cordially introduce yourselves and the stakeholders you represent, if they exist!

It is good that we introduce ourselves accordingly, so as to be familiar with the names of each other. This will help us in avoiding the risk of referring to each other as 'this one or that one'.

(*with emphasis*) Nonetheless, let me start.

My name is Edward Ndlovu, I am a member of the Cultural and Traditional Committee, the CTC. The CTC is a non-governmental organisation, an NGO (*with emphasis*) and is based in Riet Vallei. Its main objective is to promote and advocate for the norms and value systems of the African People. Our motto is '*Siyaziqhenya Ngamasiko Ethu*', which means that we are proud of our culture.

(They clap hands.)

(*EDWARD continues.*)

Now that I have introduced myself and the stakeholder that I represent, would you kindly introduce yourselves – starting with the gentleman on my right, up until the lady on my left in an anti-clockwise direction.

Gentleman, the floor is yours!

NELSON

Mr Edward, before I seize this opportunity, I would like to commend you for being part and parcel of such an august organisation and I highly commend what your organisation represents and stands for.

(*with stress*) Cultural norms and value systems are very important.

It was Marcus Garvey who argued that 'a person who does not know his history and culture, is like a tree without roots.'

Such a tree is prone and vulnerable to storms, Such a person is likely to wander and get lost.

(*They clap hands.*)

With those words of Marcus Garvey, ladies and gentlemen, consider yourself greeted.

My name is Nelson Baloyi, I am a final year master's student at the University of Cofimvaba. I am a chairperson of the King Robert's Men's Residence Forum. A residence that is based on the main campus of the University of Cofimvaba, Kingsway Campus.

The mandate of the King Robert's Men's Residence Forum is simple: Ours is to induct *male* first years from our residence into the men's culture of the University of Cofimvaba.

We want them to be Alpha males.

We want them to grow manes and be kings.

We want them to be top dogs in life.

We want them to win in every battle of life.

We want them to be top achievers in their courses.

We want them to excel in fashion and gentlemanliness.

And we want them to become beasts in sports.

Thank you very much!

MICHAEL

Brothers and Sisters! I greet you all in the name of Africa!

Africa, the land of Queendoms and Kingdoms!

(*suddenly praises his motherland*) Africa, the land of gold and silver!

My name is Michael Ngwenya.

(He proceeds to call out his clan names.)

UNgwenya,

UMntimande,

UBambolunye,

UZingabambili ngoba efuze kunina,

UKhabonina,

UMabuya bengasabuyi

UMabhodla amanzi abantukazana bebhodla utshwala

Oqhamuka esedonse ukunene noGamadze

(They all clap hands and ululate.)

I belong to the One Africa Movement.

Our movement is driving the initiative of uniting all Africans... thus to promote peace, love, unity and solidarity.

Thank you!

ITUMELENG

(*shyly*) Greetings to you all, my name is Itumeleng Tlou.

(*with a docile voice*). I am a member of the Township Domestic Affairs Movement.

This movement is mainly led by women; sisters, mothers and grandmothers.

(*she reiterates*) Females per se . . . and we all know that females are tender-loving and are natural caregivers.

In essence, we recognise that there are gender roles within a family structure; a man must be a man and a woman must be a woman.

A man must not be a woman and a woman must not be a man.

Everyone must stay in their lanes within their families. This in return guarantees peace, co-ordination and love, given a family.

Women must continue to respect their husbands!

As I submit!

BUHLEBENDALO

(*She chants.*)

Malibongweee!

COMMITTEE MEMBERS

Igama lamakhosikazi!

(*Committee members successively respond in unison.*)

BUHLEBENDALO

Igama lamakhosikazi!

COMMITTEE MEMBERS

Malibongwe!

BUHLEBENDALO

Wathinta abafazi!

COMMITTEE MEMBERS

Wathint' imbokodo!

BUHLEBENDALO

Wathint' imbokodo!

COMMITTEE MEMBERS

Wathinta abafazi!

BUHLEBENDALO

(*confidently*) *Sanibonani Nonke*!

My name is Buhlebendalo Nkosazane Ndwandwe! I am the National Chairperson of the Women's Front Unit, the NCWFU.

Our organisation strongly advocates for gender parity and equality.

In the domain of religion, we wan

In the domain of politics, we want to see women leading as presidents and ministers, not as personal assistants and secretaries for presidents and ministers.

On the table of decision-making and implementation, we want to see a proportional representation of seats, reserved both for men and women.

(She pauses, looks up, looks down and then glances over the eyes of her fellow committee members. It seems as if she was summoning strength from the roof to speak.)

(*with authority*) Ladies and gentlemen, in our organisation, we remain perplexed and puzzled by the fact that the suffix 'man' remains still in the word 'woman'

Malibongwe!

COMMITTEE MEMBERS

Igama lamakhosikazi!

(*Committee members are moved by the confidence of this woman. For a moment, they glance at each other awkwardly. Perhaps they are perplexed by the boldness of this woman. They look a bit timid.*)

'The Shinning Tower'

EDWARD

(*calmly and with a soothing tone*) Thank you very much my good friends for your decisive introductions.

You have made it obvious as to why each one of you has been chosen to come and represent your esteemed stakeholders.

Seemingly, you are all capable given your individual positions. I do not doubt that this committee will produce the desired results at its conclusion.

Nonetheless, let us get to the agenda of the day.

This is a Briefing Committee on Women Empowerment; the People's Assembly has tasked us to produce and bring forth resolutions and recommendations that seek to promote gender-parity and women-empowerment.

Noteworthy, our final resolutions and recommendations will be taken into consideration during the People's Assembly's ratification process of the Gender Parity and Women Empowerment Bill.

I, as the chairperson of this committee, will present the final resolutions and recommendations before the People's Assembly on the 25th of November.

Before we proceed with this session; I would like to set and stipulate a few rules so that we have an organised and fruitful engagement.

My fellow committee members, this procedure will unfold in this way: I will first name and explain our table rules in simple terms. I will try to be as clear as possible. You will then be free to raise your hand and ask for clarity or add something.

Let me begin.

(*He takes a deep breath before tabling the rules.*)

Rule number 1: Before you speak, please raise your hand!

Rule number 2: Please do not interrupt a person whilst he or she is speaking!

Rule number 3: When you raise your hand, please state whether it's a point of information, clarity, clarity-seeking-question, proposal, correction, addition, seconding, agreeing or disagreeing.

Rule number 4: Please learn to disagree with each other without being violently disagreeable. Agree to a point out of conviction and persuasion. Do not disagree out of spite. Debate ideas and evidence; do not debate each other out of emotions and feelings.

And that sums it up?

Are there any questions?

(*At this point, no one responds; they are all focused and looking at EDWARD.*

(*EDWARD continues.*)

Alight, if there are no questions; then allow me to continue!

My fellow committee members, our themes vary across multiple disciplines – disciplines such as history, politics, economics, sociology, psychology, physiology and anthropology. Let us draw our logic from these disciplines.

Here, we will be discussing themes of culture and gender, religion, gender as a social construction, socialisation and gender, school, gender differences, biology and gender, mass media, sexual orientation, family and sex.

We need to explore these themes so that we may clearly determine the merits and demerits that affect the quest for gender parity and women's empowerment.

Remember to say what you think and argue from any themes.

(*At this point, NELSON raises his hand and the chairman points at him.*)

NELSON

(*with a concerned face*) Chairman, this is a clarity-seeking question. (*hastily*) Why are we having this committee to begin with?

When we advocate for gender parity and women's empowerment, it seems like we do it at the expense of vilifying men. In fact, chairman (*he calls him out*), I am convinced that this Briefing Committee is nothing but a weapon formed against men!

(Michael claps his hands alone, setting an atmosphere of awkwardness.)

(Committee members laugh in return.)

(NELSON continues.)

Nonetheless, my esteemed chairman (*he calls him out*), My contention is, the rights of all persons are enshrined in our Constitution, in the Bill of Rights to be specific. Even the UN Charter promotes and protects the rights of all persons – women included.

This directly questions not only the necessity but also the legitimacy of this Briefing Committee.

For the last two decades in our country, we have been establishing gender committees. These committees are always arranged with a common agenda, namely, to promote more rights for women and to give women more powers and privileges over men.

I wouldn't be wrong at this point to state that women now have more rights than men.

MICHAEL

Through you chairman, I agree with Nelson. Women now have more rights than men.

Nowadays, if a man beats his wife and the wife opens a case, that man will be arrested in a split second. However, if the wife beats a man, and should a man decide to open a case, it is the very same police that laughs at that man whilst taking his statement.

'*Indoda eshaywa umfazi.*' Whilst giggling their lungs out.

NELSON

Whilst on that note Mr Michael; let me tell you an interesting, but yet, a very sad story.

(*He pauses and clears his throat.*)

There once lived a quiet and humble man. The man was as humble as the Lamb of Yeshua. Yet his wife was as violent as a river swollen with rain at the foothills of a mountain.

One day, his monstrous wife took a bar of steel, hit him hard and cut his head open.

The poor injured man went to the first neighbor to ask for help.

The first neighbor responded and said; 'You must take the very same bar of steel she used on you and use it on her.'

The poor man responded and said; 'Thank you.' He then left in peace.

You see, something stood out about this man; he was a man of peace, and violence was not in his blood.

Nonetheless, the poor man then decided to go to the second neighbor to ask for help.

The second neighbor responded and said; 'Go to the police station and lay charges.'

The poor man took the advice of the second neighbor.

At the police station, as the poor man was explaining to the first officer, the first officer interjected and asked to be excused to go the restroom.

Then the first officer came with a second officer and instructed the poor man to repeat his story.

As the poor man was telling the story, and before he could finish, the second officer asked to be excused as well. The first officer remained and took some notes for the statement.

After a while, the first officer took off once again and left the poor man unattended.

Before you know it, a storm of laughter unravelled in the next room.

On the day that followed, the poor man committed suicide.

'The Idiosyncrasies of Society'

MICHAEL

(He glances at NELSON.)

A very sad story . . .One day women will be the end of us.

ITUMELENG

(*She glances at MICHEAL.*)

And in most cases Michael, it is usually women who are wrong. Women sometimes can be spiteful and hormonal.

(*EDWARD braces himself for a question.*)

EDWARD

Could Kwame Nkrumah be correct when he argues in the first chapter of his book *Ghana* that 'Women by nature are quarrelsome and men by nature are polygamous?'

(*BUHLEBENDALO is seen fuming.*)

BUHLEBENDALO

(*with frustration*) My fellow committee members, I am painstakingly affected by some of the sentiments that you have shared up to now.

I am also deeply disappointed by Itumeleng, especially given that she is a woman like me.

ITUMELENG

How am I disappointing you? Please tell me, how am I disappointing?

BUHLEBENDALO

For your information, we are in the same boat sister!

(*She rolls her eyes.*)

But it seems like you are short-sighted.

ITUMELENG

What are you talking about? What boat? Please! speak clearly – we are not here for your allegories.

EDWARD

(*He reinforces his authority before chaos ensues.*)

Itumeleng, please kindly give her a chance to state her input.

(*ITUMELENG retreats immediately.*)

BUHLEBENDALO

Thank you so much chairman for protecting me.

As I continue, I have studied many literatures from different parts of the world in my lifetime. Particularly literature on gender equality and gender parity.

(*with emphasis*) And I can tell you this . . .

(*She pauses.*)

Ever since the beginning of time, women have been oppressed and suppressed.

For example, all angels in the Bible are men, even God is a man.

We are even told that Eve got a rib from a man, Adam. That it was Eve's fault for the demise of Eden. That Eve somehow conspired with the devil, a snake, to plot against Adam and God.

Before the Russian Revolution, Alexandra Feodorovna suffered the calamity of being constantly accused of conspiring with Grigori Rasputin against her husband Nikolai Alexandrovich Romanov.

Before the French Revolution, Marie Antoinette suffered the calamity of being disparaged as a 'frivolous, selfish, and immoral woman whose lavish lifestyle had increased economic inequality.'

Before Robert Mugabe's deposition, Grace Mugabe was always perceived as a 'whispering' serpent to Robert Mugabe's ears.

(*She pauses.*)

My contention is:

Throughout the ages of time, history recognises or justifies the actions of men at the expense of either vilifying women or portraying them as nonentities, conspirators, servants and aides.

As we speak, even though we have now reached a democratic era and have constitutions that promote equality, many people still believe that women are nothing but servants and aides.

Therefore, my question to all of you is 'Why should we cease the establishment of committees that seek to empower women and re-educate society in general?'

'Why should we stop? especially when women are still oppressed and suppressed?'

MICHAEL

Although I appreciate your passion Buhlebendalo, the facts remain.

(*He passionately bangs the table with his fists.*)

It was Eve who gave Adam the apple; it was Alexandra who poisoned Alexandrovich's mind; it was Marie who poisoned Louis' mind; it was Grace who poisoned Mugabe's mind; and it was Delilah who cut Samson's hair and compromised him.

'The Serpent and the Apple'

BUHLEBENDALO

(*She addresses MICHAEL.*)

Point of information chairman! Although Michael's poetry is as good as gold (she rolls her eyes), I think he needs to hear this.

(*She continues.*)

Mr Michael (*calling him out*), Samson was nothing but a cheat.

Samson was involved with three women: a woman from Timnah, a woman from Gaza and also Delilah. With such promiscuous behaviour, you are bound to eventually get what's coming for you. In fact, Samson had an option not to be with Delilah on that day, or ever. He was a married man for Christ's sake!

ITUMELENG

From my side, what a man does outside is none of my concern.

(*rolling her eyes*) As long as he comes back home, takes care of me, takes care of his children and takes care of his family.

NELSON

I agree with Itumeleng, let men be!

EDWARD, MICHAEL and ITUMELENG

(*They speak in unison.*)

Let men be!

MICHAEL

Africans with their wisdom realised a long time ago that men by nature are polygamous! That is why they recognised and also allowed polygamous marriages to exist.

As long as the first wife has given the go-ahead for her husband to marry a second, third, fourth or fifth wife.

I see no problem with polygamy!

BUHLEBENDALO

But chairman, that was then. Times have changed. The reckless act of involving yourself in multiple sexual relationships will cost you your life nowadays. I have a question: Why is it that when a man has a lot of girlfriends he is referred to as '*Isoka*', but if a woman dares to have a lot of boyfriends, she risks being called '*isfebe*'?

Can you ever imagine a situation where it would be said: 'A woman who once had 700 husbands and 300 concubines'?

Can you?

(No one responds.)

Nonetheless, one man in history did and today he is being praised as the wisest of them all.

(She pauses a bit and then continues.)

We live in a sick world where men are in a frenzy over polygamy but frown at polyandry.

We live in a sick world where men cheat and expect to be forgiven. But if a woman cheats, it becomes another story.

Chairman, something is fundamentally wrong with the psyche of our society and it must be fixed. Clearly, this is not a misdiagnosis, thorough counseling and therapy is needed.

EDWARD

(He calls her out.)

Ms Buhlebendalo!

NELSON

(He interrupts.)

Umm, chairman, before you speak, I just want to address something quickly.

I for one will rather choose a foolish virgin than marry a Mary Magdalene.

In fact, give me all ten virgins; the foolish and the wise!

(They all burst into laughter, except for BUHLEBENDALO.)

'Commiseration'

MICHAEL

On a point of fact, I am with Nelson on that one. If a woman cheats or sleeps around, she loses her value as a woman.

To put it in layman's terms, it is only a fool who buys a car with a high mileage. Such a car will give you problems.

(They all burst into laughter, except for BUHLEBENDALO.)

BUHLEBENDALO

(irritated) May I ask, what is funny?

(They cease to laugh.)

If this committee is here for comedy, then I am in the wrong place.

EDWARD

(He calms her down.)

No, Ms Buhlebendalo! You are in the right place.

BUHLEBENDALO

(She commands with authority.)

Listen to me and listen attentively:

Whilst you are busy giggling your lungs out, Thousands and thousands of women are being trafficked for sex slavery.

Just like the slaves, they are being displayed, auctioned and sold at brothels.

Others are being kept as sex toys in the houses of rich men.

Toddlers and infants are being raped by delusional people who believe that 'virginity cleanses the soul.'

You see chairman, the problem starts when we objectify women.

Today a slenderer woman is called a sedan, whilst a thick-boned woman is called an SUV, a truck or Code 14.

I must add that these shameless body-shaming nukes go hand-in-glove with stereotypes.

Others believe that a slenderer woman is good for summer.

On the other hand, some believe that a thick-boned woman is good for winter.

You would swear that some men think with their genitals.

MICHAEL

Ms Buhlebendalo, I have a question for you. What is your take on women who falsely accuse men of rape?

NELSON

Good question!

BUHLEBENDALO

Before I answer this question Michael, I just want to go back to your absurd notion about cheating.

Chiefly, I do not condone cheating, or any act of sexual promiscuity. It is immoral and disgusting. Whether done by a man or a woman, cheating is never justified.

And again, it is never justified to kill your partner because he or she cheated.

Rather leave if you do not wish to continue with the relationship anymore. Or forgive them and continue with the relationship if you find it in your heart to do so.

However, should you decide to take matters into your own hands and break the law. Just know that it is a matter of time before the mighty hand of the law snatches you.

Coming to your question Michael, women who falsely accuse men of rape must be arrested as well.

Men who rape must be arrested.

Women who rape must be arrested.

Rape is a crime and false accusation of rape is a crime. Therefore; the mighty sword of law must never be lenient on those who undermine its slash.

(They all clap hands.)

NELSON

Fair enough! I have another question Ms Buhlebendalo.

BUHLEBENDALO

(*smiling*) Hopefully, you won't ask me a misogynistic question.

NELSON

(*with an awkward smile*) No, I won't. Nonetheless, here is my question: What becomes of a man who has been exonerated but has served a portion or a full sentence for his 'supposed crime'?

BUHLEBENDALO

(*sighs*) Sadly, what is done cannot be undone. Whatever the consequence, the falsely accused man will never retrieve his lost years of freedom. One can never imagine his pain and the psychological implications of wandering in a cell for a crime he did not commit. It's terrible. However, in this scenario, both the accuser and the judiciary have a responsibility.

NELSON

(*He looks at her curiously.*)

What is the responsibility of the accuser? What is the responsibility of the judiciary regarding the accuser? What is the responsibility of the judiciary regarding the falsely accused?

Must the judiciary or the state be held accountable in any way?

BUHLEBENDALO

In this scenario, the accuser must issue a statement of apology.

NELSON

Excuse me, an apology did not retrieve four decades that Anthony Broadwater lost wandering in jail for a crime of rape he did not commit.

There are many cases of this kind, and I can assure you that there are men who are rotting in jail for crimes they did not commit. Some of them will be exonerated and some of them will stay in jail.

Because of false accusations of rape, many have lost their livelihoods.

Many have lost their jobs.

Many have lost their erstwhile friends.

Many have been subjected to the torment of social exclusion.

Many have been maltreated by their family members.

The fact is that no one wants to be associated with someone who is being accused of rape.

Unfortunately, some people live with this horrific stigma for the rest of their lives.

Believe me, I do not condone rape or sexual assaults in any way. However, I speak for those who are falsely accused. An apology is not enough for them; they also deserve justice.

BUHLEBENDALO

(*drawing her eyebrows*) My fellow committee members, our Constitution must protect us like an eagle protecting its nest. We are all under the wings of law, therefore, there must be justice for everyone who has been wronged in any way.

In the case of false accusation of rape and exoneration, if the falsely accused requires a formal apology from the accuser, perhaps for forgiveness and finding closure, (*waving her hands*) it then becomes the accuser's responsibility to apologise.

MICHAEL

What if the accuser refuses to issue an apology?

ITUMELENG

Good question! What happens then?

(They all nod.)

BUHLEBENDALO

Then the court must note and consider that the accuser refused to issue an apology to a person whom she falsely accused.

EDWARD

(EDWARD points at her with his pen.)

How does the court come into this? How did we get there? The last time I checked we were still talking about apologies.

(They all laugh.)

BUHLEBENDALO

Exactly where I was getting to in answering Nelson on his question of responsibilities by the state and the judiciary.

As I stated, everyone must be protected by the wings of the law.

The falsely accused may lay charges against the accuser and may also sue the accuser for defamatory and perversion of the course of justice if he or she wishes to. The falsely accused may not only sue the accuser but may also sue the state for a negligent investigation.

NELSON

Fair enough, however, over the years, social scientists have diagnosed a new virus, particularly in the favelas, ghettos and townships. This virus is called, rape extortion and has infected both the poor and the rich.

'The Rule of Law'

EDWARD

Excuse my interference, please explain before this committee, what is rape extortion?

NELSON

The concept of rape extortion is closely related to the concept of false accusation. The similarity that binds them is the word 'false.' However, rape extortion involves money, and illegal involves the means of extracting money. Illegal means, for instance, the use of threats and intimidation.

In the case of rape extortion, you have partner A who had consensual sex with partner B. However, partner A subsequently demands money from partner B or vice versa. Usually, partner A is aware that partner B has money, access to resources or some form of power.

Partner A then sets demands for partner B, usually including the amount of money needed and the day it is needed. If partner B does not meet the demands stipulated by partner A, partner A then threatens to open a case of rape or to expose partner B before the public.

In most cases, partner B ends up yielding to the demands of partner A – not out of choice – but out of fear of being accused of rape and the consequences that accompany such an accusation.

I can assure you, it's a very ugly situation.

MICHAEL

That is very true, I have seen instances where others go to the extent of laying charges of rape if the other party refuses to pay the money.

NELSON

To add on that Michael, others go ahead and lay charges and then demand money to drop the charges – and in most cases, this is done by women.

EDWARD

As Ms Buhlebendalo enlightened us, I think we have to go back once more to the Rule of Law. If a person is being threatened and intimidated to take out money, I think the best option for dealing with this situation, is to alert the authorities.

MICHAEL

To add to that chairman, if there is sufficient evidence that implicates the rape extortionist beyond any reasonable doubt, the victim must lay charges of intimidation and defamation so that the criminal may be charged and prosecuted. It will set an example and warning other rape extortionists and possible rape extortionists.

BUHLEBENDALO

(*She raises her hand.*)

Excuse me, chairman I have a point of information.

EDWARD

(*He points at her.*)

Go on Ms Buhlebendalo.

BUHLEBENDALO

Nelson touched on something that covers the scope of my research. I think there is a dialectical link between poverty and rape extortion.

ITUMELENG

What does poverty have to do with rape extortion? Are you trying to justify rape extortion in any way?

EDWARD

Ms Itumeleng, please give her a chance to explain.

BUHLEBENDALO

Thank you chairman for protecting me!

Let me proceed. To understand a certain problem comprehensively, one has to understand its roots – what we call the root of a problem. Once we understand the root of a problem, not only will we be able to understand the problem, but we will also be able to come up with solutions for that problem and prevent it from repeating itself.

MICHAEL

I still do not understand how poverty finds itself in the phenomenon of rape extortion.

(*he instructs*) Can you please get straight to the point ma'am?

BUHLEBENDALO

That is the problem, isn't it? We always want to cut to the chase about a certain aspect without fully understanding its characteristics. Here I am, giving you an equation of studying and understanding aspects, but you want me to give you an answer already without me carrying you through a logical process. Please, allow me to defend my point since I am the one who brought it up for discussion.

EDWARD

(*EDWARD speaks to all and gives direction.*)

My fellow committee members, let us allow her to carry us through her logic. The table is yours Ms Buhlebendalo.

BUHLEBENDALO

Thank you once again, chairman. Let me then proceed.

The crime of rape extortion is quite rife in favelas, ghettos and townships – and guess what, that's where we always find escalating poverty rates.

In most cases, women who commit the crime of rape extortion have low self-esteem; they lack self-confidence, and somewhere, somehow poverty is involved.

They will do anything to get money and redeem their situations. Sadly, whatever extortion money they can get, can only redeem their circumstances temporarily.

EDWARD

Ms Buhlebendalo, it is not only poverty that pushes people to commit the crime of rape extortion – even rich people are possible suspects. What is your take on that?

BUHLEBENDALO

I am not saying that poverty is the only factor that pushes people to commit the crime of rape extortion. My fellow committee members, it is always inadequate to look at a particular aspect from a singular point of view. We must always use multiple lenses to interpret any situation. Perhaps we may then arrive at an accurate conclusion.

I contend that many people commit the crime of rape extortion because of other reasons or ulterior motives.

It could be out of spite or greediness. Also, others may be sent to set a trap for you.

My brothers and sisters, we live in a sick world. My advice to men is to be careful with whom you share a bed.

EDWARD

Fair enough!

(*He pauses.*)

My fellow committee members, I believe that lying in general should be made a crime.

(*with a smile*) Perhaps this will help to curb the problem of rape extortion.

MICHAEL

(*laughing*) My esteemed chairman, when you deliver our report before the People's Assembly, please propose the 'Lying Bill.' This bill must be tabled, debated and passed as an act, The 'Lying Act'!

ITUMELENG

I agree with you Michael, we are tired of being lied to; people lie a lot around here, especially these uppity women and politicians.

(*BUHLEBENDALO rolls her eyes out of irritation.*)

NELSON

I cannot wait for the Lying Bill to be passed as an act. That will be my weapon in building up a strong case.

There is someone that I want to deal with, decisively!

ITUMELENG

Who?

NELSON

My ex-girlfriend!

ITUMELENG

(*asks curiously*) What did she do?

NELSON

She once told me that 'we will die together like Romeo and Juliet.'

ITUMELENG

Where is she now? what happened?

NELSON

(*rolling his eyes*) Duh, obviously she was lying. Today I am as single as a pringle.

(They all laugh hysterically.)

EDWARD

You guys want to throw me into the lion's den. I am still too young to die. Imagine proposing a bill about lying before lying prefects.

(They all laugh.)

Nonetheless, back to business.

(*pointing at her with his pen*) Ms Buhlebendalo, I just want to take you back a little bit, where you said and I quote; 'something is fundamentally wrong.'

I agree with you, something is fundamentally wrong.

My questions are:

What is the initial problem?

What causes the moral and psychological degradation of our societies?

What is it that affects the psyche of our society?

(He pauses and waits for an answer, but no one answers.

(He goes on.)

I will tell you:

We have a group of women called feminists!

They are nothing but a toxic brigade!

These women are nothing but a bunch of pathological liars who masquerade as gender activists!

They are nothing but a bunch of angry women who spring out of failed relationships.

They are bitter con artists who use the real problem of gender-based violence and femicide as an asset to maximise their profits.

They establish NPOs, but in reality, they are driven by profit. If the profit margin is low, they do not mind protesting naked.

On the other hand, they have exported Western ideas of how a man should act, react and conduct himself.

Their agenda is against an African man. And they will not rest until an African man is gender-neutral.

Sadly, they have succeeded in manipulating and implementing these ideas. Theirs is to reduce an African man into docility.

This toxic group has succeeded in making an African man weak.

Lately, an African man had no say in his household. If an African man stipulates rules in his house, feminists call him controlling, abusive and narcissistic.

These women want to be wives, but they refuse to do wives' duties.

I pity a man who will marry a feminist, for there will be two bulls in one kraal.

'The Quest'

BUHLEBENDALO

(*She raises her hand*).

Chairman, I have a question seeking clarity on an issue.

EDWARD

(He points at her with his pen once more)

Please, go on Ms Buhlebendalo!

BUHLEBENDALO

(She calls out EDWARD.)

Mr Edward!

EDWARD

(EDWARD replies.)

Yes, ma'am!

BUHLEBENDALO

Can you please define the word 'toxic' before this committee?

EDWARD

The word toxic refers to something that has to do with poison.

BUHLEBENDALO

Okay, now can you please explain the meaning of pathology?

EDWARD

Ms Buhlebendalo, where are these questions going?

BUHLEBENDALO

My dear sir, please answer the question!

EDWARD

Okay, according to my books, pathology has something to do with lying.

BUHLEBENDALO

If I am getting you correctly, according to your books, feminists are a 'bunch' of poisonous women who have something to do with lying. Correct?

EDWARD

(*EDWARD replies insistently.*)

Correct, and I maintain that!

BUHLEBENDALO

I put it to you, my dear sir that you are displaying a lot of ignorance and intellectual dwarfism. To add to that, this says a lot about the content of your character. Unfortunately, you are not the only one who harbours such dangerous views about the whole feminist movement.

EDWARD

Okay, Ms All-Knowing, please enlighten me; how am I being ignorant?

BUHLEBENDALO

Firstly, your logic is based on faulty generalisations. In the worst scenario, you throw dangerous words into your argument without even knowing their normative definitions.

For example, your answer on defining pathology is quite laughable. If I was your teacher, I would give you a zero with ears and carve it with a 'come-and-see-me-after-class' instruction.

EDWARD

Okay Ms All-Knowing, please teach me, what is pathology.

BUHLEBENDALO

I will tell you.

Pathology is a branch of medical sciences that involves the study and diagnosis of diseases through the examination of surgically removed organs, tissues, bodily fluids, and in some cases, the whole body.

This is a major root definition of the word ‘pathology’, however, it can be used and traded to other disciplines, such as pathophysiology, cardiomyopathy and psychiatry.

Nonetheless, I suggest that you use the root word of pathology in ‘pathological liar’ in the context of psychology and psychiatry.

In psychology and psychiatry, pathological lying is a symptom of various personality disorders, including anti-social, narcissistic, and histrionic personality disorders.

So according to your books, feminists are a bunch of poisonous women who suffer from mental disorders. Correct?

EDWARD

Hold it right there, you are twisting my words. I never said that!

BUHLEBENDALO

Did you or did you not use the word ‘toxic’ in your diction, which refers to poison? Yes, or no?

EDWARD

(*mumbles*) Ms Buhlebendalo . . .

BUHLEBENDALO

(*She interjects before he can finish.*

(*She then questions EDWARD sternly.*)

Sir, answer my question! Did you or did you not use the word 'toxic' in your diction which refers to poison? Yes, or no?

EDWARD

Yes, I did!

BUHLEBENDALO

Did you or did you not use the word 'pathological' in your diction?

Yes, or no?

EDWARD

Yes, I did!

BUHLEBENDALO

Now, here is my point.

Stop using words without knowing their definitive meanings, especially dangerous words, and especially if you are sitting in a position of authority or power. You risk triggering something that you may not be able to control.

Using dangerous words in general is dangerous.

The word '*Untermensch*' resulted in the genocide of more than six million people in Nazi Germany.

The word 'dissidents' resulted in a genocide of more than 20 thousand people in Zimbabwe.

The word 'cockroaches' resulted in a genocide of more than 800 thousand people in Rwanda.

Words such as ‘faggot’, ‘fag’, ‘she-male’, ‘he-she’ and ‘tranny’ have cost the lives of many people from the homosexual community.

Another thing, twice you called me Ms ‘All-Knowing’. If the shoe fits, wear it. If I was all-knowing, I wouldn’t be reading every day. If I was all-knowing, I would stop hunting for knowledge every day. But I can tell you this, I never speak about something unless I know it. If I do not know something, I listen. And if I do not understand, I ask questions.

EDWARD

Okay then, excuse my ignorance. I have another question.

BUHLEBENDALO

(*in a firm tone*) Go ahead, ask!

EDWARD

You mentioned that my argument is based on faulty generalisations. My question is: How is my argument general, especially when everybody knows the true agenda of feminists?

BUHLEBENDALO

Mr Edward, I just want to get something correct. When you say everybody, do you also count the views of a four-year-old in kindergarten?

EDWARD

Obviously not!

BUHLEBENDALO

Okay, now tell me, who is everybody or what is everybody? Do you mean the entire world population of eight billion human species?

EDWARD

(*mumbling*) I mean everybody, as in 'everyone'. All those here know what I am talking about.

BUHLEBENDALO

The question is, do you even know what you are really talking about? You cannot come here and just say 'everybody' – everybody could be anyone – and that's how general your argument is.

And I must warn you again, making general and sweeping statements is also dangerous. Do you know why? I will tell you! Because every Tom, Dick and Harry who doesn't base their argument on facts, like you, always mistakes general arguments for truths.

For example, you said that feminists are a bunch of angry women who spring out of failed relationships and that they establish NPOs, but in reality are driven by profits.

Mr. Edward, this is a very dangerous argument. First and foremost, I know a lot of women who have maintained and are maintaining stable and healthy relationships and are staunch feminists at the same time. These are women who are genuinely prepared to fight the scourge of patriarchy wherever it may be. These women are prepared to fight against gender inequality wherever it may be, and they are not driven by profits.

People who claim that they are fighting for a certain cause, while in reality are fighting for their stomachs, are nothing but criminals. Any person who masquerades under the banner of the feminist movement, whilst in reality is driven by profits, is nothing but a criminal. Therefore, do not tell me about criminals, rather, tell me about true feminists. Feminists who are prepared to fight gender inequality and patriarchy wherever it may be.

And I can assure you, the problem of patriarchy is an international problem. Wherever you may go, in any part of the world, stereotypes and prejudices against women are evident. That is why the feminist movement is not just a national or a continental movement, rather, it is an international movement. That is why I do not take your remarks seriously when you say that feminism is a weapon formed against African men.

On the other hand, I must reiterate that women have been fighting for their rights since the beginning of time. At some point in the struggle, one ought to risk being offensive or take an offensive position to convince or defeat the enemy. I believe that to provoke society to think or act, one must risk being offensive.

Many governments across the world are deaf to the plight of women. And if they respond, they give mere lip service. It's been too long since women have been fighting for their rights if needs be, and if it will get any government to listen or respond, let them protest naked.

NELSON

To some extent, I agree with you Ms Buhlebendalo. However, I suggest that your argument is biased.

BUHLEBENDALO

How is it biased?

NELSON

It seems like your argument subjectively clings to the side of women. What about men? Are you ever going to address their issues? If indeed the whole synopsis of the struggle against gender parity and women empowerment is not a weapon formed against men, I think that at some point, we also need to address issues faced by men.

My fellow committee members, I put it to you; men suffer too. However, their personal, economic, social and political struggles are overlooked.

'Babylon'

For example, most people who are in jail are men.

Most people who are in jail for crimes they didn't commit are men.

Most people who are homeless are men.

Most people who commit suicide are men.

Most people who violently commit suicide are men.

Most people who drop out of school are men.

Most people who do manual labour are men.

Most people who die on duty are men.

Most people who die in wars are men.

Most people who suffer from depression are men.

Most people who are victims of alcohol and drug abuse are men.

(*They all clap hands.*)

MICHAEL

It's true that men also go through a lot, however, society encourages them to conceal their truest emotions. It seems like society in general favours and supports women over men.

NELSON

(*He calls out the chairman.*)

Mr Chairman, I have a question! Why is it that in most cases, a man is expected to pay for child support? Are children solely reproduced by men?

Why is it that in most cases, it is women who win children's custody?

MICHAEL

Chairman, as I stated before, women have more rights than men.

This means that our society and courts favour women over men. According to legend, all animals are equal, but some animals are more equal than others. And this is what we are seeing when it comes to gender politics.

On the other hand, I am perplexed by the contradictions of the feminists brigade. These are the very same people who advocate for women's empowerment. However, at the end of the month, some of them have the nerve to ask men for money. At least, the expectation that a man should provide financially and otherwise remains.

(*draws his eyebrows*) What happened to fairness? What happened to the advocacy of gender parity and equality?

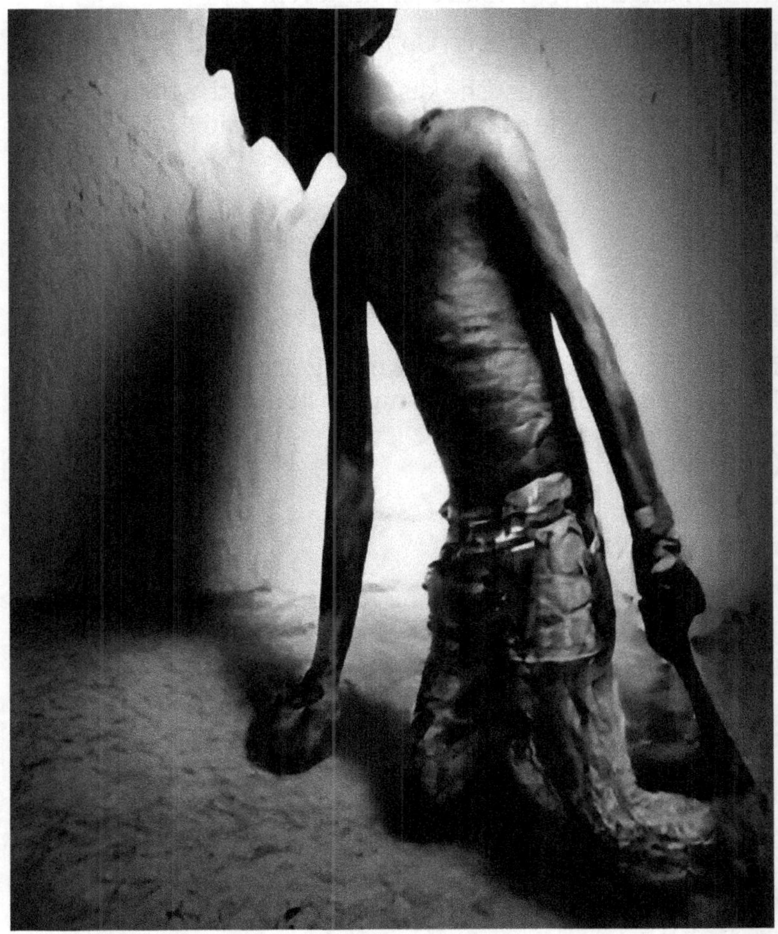

'Dejection'

NELSON

Through you, Mr Chairman, it is like Michael is reading my mind. Out there are families who encourage their girls to marry rich men. That is why other women do not want to go to school or use their skills to start businesses. That is why other women do not bother to carve and nourish their talents. For them, marrying a rich man is an achievement.

I once heard a story about a woman who found a rich man.

It is said that the day she discovered that the man she was dating was rich, she called her mother and said:

'Mama, ndiwufumen' umsebenzi'

(They all laugh.)

ITUMELENG

If it was me, Nelson, I was not only going to call my mother, I was going to call my entire family including my neighbors.

(*They all laugh again.*)

BUHLEBENDALO

(*She raises her hand.*)

Point of information chairman!

EDWARD

(*He instructs.*)

Go on Ms Buhlebendalo!

BUHLEBENDALO

(*She begins her narration.*)

I have been listening to every single one of you attentively of course. I must attest, I find some of your sentiments quite amusing. However, let me share some insights about a few issues.

(She pauses and then begins.)

The only difference between men and women is through biology.

What is my contention?

I contend that a lot of people confuse or use the concepts of sex and gender interchangeably without understanding what they mean. They have no inkling of their normative definitions.

(She pauses a bit and then proceeds to ask a rhetorical question.)

What is sex?

The concept of sex refers to the anatomical and physiological differences between males and females and includes both primary and secondary sexual characteristics.

Primary sexual characteristics refer to the anatomical and physiological differences between a male and a female; a male has a penis and a scrotum whilst a female has a vagina and a uterus.

Secondary sexual characteristics develop during the stage of puberty. Males begin to develop deeper voices and grow facial hairs. Females, on the other hand, begin to grow larger breasts and their hips begin to widen.

Gender refers to the cultural differences of people based on their sex. In those differences, there are perceptions of what a man is expected to do and what a woman is expected to do.

Regarding men, we call those perceptions masculinity – usually toxic.

For women, we call those perceptions femininity – also toxic.

My point is that gender is a social construct – it has nothing to do with physiology. It is society over the years that has constructed and enforced rules that define and stipulate a dichotomy between a man and a woman.

Ladies and gentlemen; we have a duty here.

(*She bangs the table with a clenched fist.*)

Ours is to deconstruct and detox society from this deadly poison. And I must warn you about this poison. This poison comes in a golden cup and we have all drank from it.

In most cases, we have no clue when we drink it. Our eyes are only enticed by this indefinable and celestial golden cup. Before we know it, we have drunk the poison.

EDWARD

(*asks curiously*) Ms. Buhlebendalo, what is this poison that you are talking about?

BUHLEBENDALO

My fellow committee members, this poison involves mainly two elements: toxic masculinity and toxic femininity. Both males and females gobble this poison until adolescence, and both men and women gobble this poison until their last days on Earth.

Sadly, they never die without passing the 'know-how mixture' of this poison to their successive generations.

(*She realises that her fellow committee members are a bit confused, she pauses and then continues.*)

My dear friends, picture it this way.

From the moment we are born, we are introduced and accustomed to a society that constitutes of a clear distinction between men and women.

From the moment we are born, we are introduced and accustomed to cultural and social characteristics that will define us either as 'men' or 'women.'

For example, a boy child is told not to cry so that he may grow up to be a strong man.

On the other hand, a girl child is taught how to wash dishes at a very tender age.

EDWARD

(*He praises BUHLEBENDALO*)

You make some strong insights Ms Buhlebendalo and I commend you for your intellect. However, I have a question for you.

(*clears his throat*) My question is, where and how do we begin to detox society from this deadly poison?

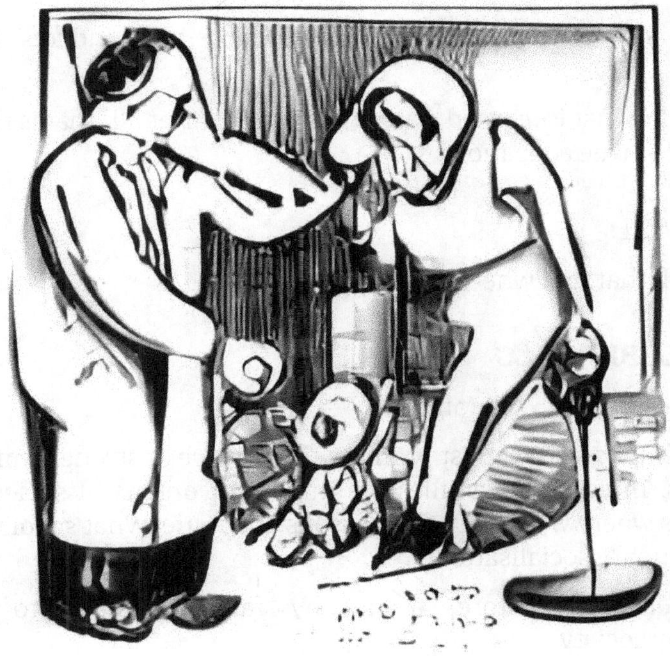

'Poison, Toxicity and Death'

BUHLEBENDALO

(*calls out EDWARD passionately*) Mr. Edward, here is a clear mandate:

(She now goes through her mandate.)

We need to re-teach society.

Let society understand that anything that has not been scientifically proven is nothing but a theory.

Let society understand that anything that has not been scientifically proven is nothing but a bubble full of air – and that it's a matter of time before it bursts into nothingness.

Let society understand that the perceptions that accompany the concepts of gender and gender roles are nothing but a social construction.

(with stress) A systematic construction that inducts us into toxicity.

Anything that is learned, can be unlearned. After all, that is the power of true education.

EDWARD

I get all that, but where do we start?

BUHLEBENDALO

We need to start with families.

(*with emphasis*) We must promote the essence of strong family values. In essence, families are important organs of society. That is where we get our first lessons about life. What scholars call primary socialisation.

(*she adds*) Therefore, a healthy family equates to a healthy society.

If we allow families to preach and cement stereotypes and prejudices, we will have no one to blame but ourselves for allowing stereotypes and prejudices to thrive in society.

Therefore, let us encourage families to teach their children good values and norm systems.

There is no such thing as a boy or a man must not cry. Naturally, human beings cry, boys and men are human beings. Then why shouldn't they cry?

In fact, crying is healthy. Crying allows us to release stress and emotional pain.

Therefore, the boy child must not be taught how to be a man. Instead, he must be taught how to be human.

The girl child must not be taught how to be a woman. Instead, she must be taught how to be human.

All humans must be taught how to be humane.

NELSON

My esteemed Mr Chairman, I do not think that it is necessary to encourage young boys to cry and wash dishes. It is nothing but a recipe for disaster. We cannot create a society of weak men who cry and wash dishes.

We must teach our young boys how to man up!

I insist we must teach our young boys how to be men.

MICHAEL

I agree with Nelson. We must encourage our young boys to have balls of steel.

BUHLEBENDALO

(*agitatedly*) Through you chairman. If that is the case, let us also encourage young girls to have breasts of steel.

NELSON

Why? So that they can grow up and disrespect men?

BUHLEBENDALO

No! So that they can learn to stand up for themselves.

NELSON

By standing up you mean disrespecting men. Right? And again Ms Buhlebendalo, you must remember that this is Africa, we have our own values and norms. And they must be respected and preserved at all costs.

MICHAEL

To add on that, she must not indoctrinate us with her Western philosophies!

BUHLEBENDALO

(*firmly*) If encouraging young women to get educated is a Western philosophy, then I am part of that agenda.

If encouraging young women to create sustainable and sound careers for themselves is a Western philosophy, then I am part of that agenda.

If encouraging families to preach and teach moral values and norms is a Western philosophy, then I am part of that agenda.

If encouraging women to extract themselves from abusive relationships is a Western philosophy, then I am part of that agenda.

ITUMELENG

My fellow committee members, allow me to say this. I think Buhlebendalo belongs to that toxic brigade that you have been talking about, the feminists. She is one of those women who disrespect men. She is part of that agenda.

BUHLEBENDALO

(*angrily*) Don't you dare label and disrespect me. Don't you dare!

If that is the case, you Itumeleng belong to that branch of fragile women who cannot stand up for themselves.

ITUMELENG

Just because you disrespect your man, it does not give you the right to disrespect everyone. One can read through your character that you are one of those women who disrespect men.

EDWARD

(*in a conciliatory tone*) Ladies! Ladies!

Please do not fight, we came here to find solutions.

BUHLEBENDALO

But Edward, you allowed her to speak to me however she wanted. And you didn't reprimand her.

One of the rules you stipulated is that people must allow ideas and evidence to be debated instead of feelings and emotions.

EDWARD

My humblest apologies Buhlebendalo; I will never allow such a situation again.

(At this point, ITUMELENG stands up and slowly moves towards the centre of the stage. She is about to deliver an emotional yet moving soliloquy and is tearful.)

ITUMELENG

(*loudly – at the top of her lungs*) Enough! Enough! Enough!

(She begins her narration.)

I was only 16 years old when my uncle raped me.

People say that blood is thicker than water, but I can tell you that sometimes water is cleaner than blood.

I never thought that my own family – my blood, my uncle – would one day do this to me.

(She continues with her narration.)

One day when I was alone in the house, I heard a door opening.

Quickly, I rushed to the door.

It was my uncle. Sadly, he was very drunk, his usual state.

'Can you please dish up some food for me,' he asked.

'Okay Malume,' I responded.

I stood up and went to the kitchen.

There I was, dishing up some food for him, hymning my beautiful song.

(She begins to sing an emotional African melody.)

'*Thula thu thula mama thula sana, thulu mam' uzobuya ekuseni*'

Amidst a soothing moment; amidst of my absentmindedness and hymns; I felt a hand touching my behind.

Little did I know that it was the hand of the devil, Lucifer himself, my uncle, my family, and my blood.

My uncle pulled my leggings down.

I tried to resist you see, but his testosterone was too powerful for me.

He then struck me and held my head still against the plate of the stove. Luckily, the stove was off.

I tried to scream, but then he aggressively bashed my head against the plate of the stove. And my head remained still in his awkward grip.

'If you try that again, I will turn on the stove and burn this pretty face of yours,' he said.

All that I could do under the circumstances was to sob and bleed.

When he was done with his devilish act, he whispered in my ears like a serpent and said. 'If you tell anyone, I will kill you.'

He might not have killed me that day, but I can assure you that a part of me died that day.

(*with anger and frustration*) He killed my innocence for Chrissake!

I lost my virginity to a rapist, my own blood, my family, my uncle, a criminal.

(*she looks up in prayer*) Dear God, thank you for avenging me.

(*with an awkward smile*) At least I have a grave to spit on today.

Over the years, I sat down and kept quiet about it.

(*adamantly*) But not anymore, I refuse to sit down!

Today I am standing up and I am standing up with my mouth wide open.

I am standing up with a clear conscious.

Not only for me but for everyone who is a survivor.

Stand up too!

(At this point, ITUMELENG goes back to her chair. She sits next to a teary and emotional NELSON. Seemingly, his emotions are overwhelming him. Apparently, he is drowning in a pool of pain and sorrow.

(He can't help but give ITUMELENG a tight hug. He begins to sob over her shoulder and together they begin to sob.

(BUHLEBENDALO stands up and moves towards the centre of the stage. She delivers a powerful soliloquy. Hers is to encourage

women; hers is to comfort ITUMELENG; hers is to comfort all women).

BUHLEBENDALO

My name is Buhlebendalo Nkosazane Ndwandwe.

I am a woman.

A very proud woman.

I am not an aide to a man.

You may try and omit me from history, but history has no blank pages.

When men were carrying sticks and walking with dogs around the bush down in the valley of Mesopotamia, we women discovered agriculture.

We are scientists by nature.

We observe, calculate and implement.

You may ignore our roles and significance but know that a woman is the first teacher of a child

We are mothers of nations.

My name is Buhlebendalo Nkosazane Ndwandwe.

I am born of queens, saints and warriors.

I am the offspring of Queen Nzinga of Ndongo and Matamba; an astute diplomat and a visionary military leader.

I am the child of Mother Teresa.

I dedicate my life to nurture and care for the dejected and rejected, for my heart is of gold,

I am the daughter of Mbuya Nehanda – a woman who masterminded the first Chimurenga, down in the Mountains of the Kingdom of Zimbabwe.

I was born of intellectuals, warriors, educators and great mathematicians.

I am born of thinkers – Marie Curie, Indira Gandhi, Maya Angelou, Michelle Obama, Oprah Winfrey, Sojourner Truth, Rosa Parks and Susan B. Anthony.

I am every woman!

The End

The Lexicon of Poison

This section contains:

1. Elements of a play you need to understand plays in general.
2. The vocabulary used in the play *Poison* (glossary).
3. The vernacular vocabulary you need to understand to fully grasp the main and minor plots of *Poison* (vernacular).
4. The structural elements of a plot.
5. Style, diction, syntax and figures of speech.

1. Elements of a play you need to understand plays in general

acts: The different parts of a play.

antagonist: In a drama or narrative, the principal opponent of the main character.

anti-climax: A disappointing end to an exciting or impressive series of events.

cast: A group of actors and actresses performing in a play or movie.

characters: The people who the play is all about.

characterisation: The creation or construction of a fictional character.

climax: The most intense or exciting part of the story.

conflict: A struggle between the antagonist and the protagonist.

costumes: The clothes, accessories and hairdos worn by the actors and actresses.

dialogue: A conversation between two or more people, or speech that is written down as part of a piece of narrative text.

director: A professional who supervises the actors and actresses.

drama: A play, movie, or television production with a serious tone or subject.

dramatic effect: A phenomenon that unfolds on stage and grabs the audience's attention.

dramatic purpose: Every line, dialogue, soliloquy and action must have a purpose in drama. This is called a dramatic purpose.

dramatic irony: When the audience or the reader knows more about the situation and what is happening than the characters on stage.

dramatic structure: The way a play is put together.

euphemism: A mild expression or polite word substituted for one considered to be too harsh or blunt when referring to something unpleasant or embarrassing.

exposition: The beginning of the story.

falling action: When the conflict in a drama begins to be resolved.

figurative language: A way of expressing oneself that does not use a word's strict or realistic language.

irony: When a statement, line, phrase or situation has an ultimate meaning that is different from the literal meaning.

main plot: The most important story that the play tells us.

metaphor: A figure of speech that uses one aspect to describe another aspect.

minor characters: The supporting cast.

mood: The atmosphere or the emotions of characters.

playwright: A person who writes plays.

plot: The main events that take place in the play.

props: Short for 'properties'; the property of the character who uses them on stage.

protagonist: The main character in a play.

protest theatre: A form of political theatre that uses performance to raise awareness of social and political issues.

resolution: Also known as denouement or conclusion; the final part of a play where a resolution or conclusion is reached.

rising action: The events of conflict in a play that culminate towards a climax.

sarcasm: The use of irony to mock or show disgruntlement.

scenes: A division of an act presenting continuous action in one place.

set: An arrangement of scenery and properties to depict where the play takes place.

setting: Where and when the play takes place.

soliloquy: When the character speaks his/her thoughts aloud. Note, the spoken word may be directed to the audience as well.

sub-plot: An event or a story that is told along with the main story.

symbol: Something that stands for or represents something.

stage directions: Instructions written into the script of a play, showing the ways of how actors and actresses must act, speak and project their voices.

themes: The main ideas in a play.

tone: A literary device that reflects the writer's attitude toward the subject matter or audience of literary work.

2. The vocabulary used in the play *Poison* (glossary)

advocate: A person (as a lawyer) who works and argues in support of another's cause/to support a cause.

agenda: A list of items to be discussed at a formal meeting.

aide: An assistant to an important person, especially a political person.

allegory: A story, poem, or picture that can be interpreted to reveal a hidden meaning, typically a moral or a political one.

august: To be respected and impressive.

biased: Unfairly prejudiced for or against someone or something.

Bill of Rights: A document that enshrines the rights of all people in our country and affirms the democratic values of human dignity, equality and freedom.

brothel: A house/building where men visit prostitutes.

cardiomyopathy: A chronic disease of the heart muscle.

calamity: An event causing great and often sudden damage or distress; a disaster.

cease: To come to or bring to an end.

compromise: An intentional violation.

conceal: To not allow to be seen; to hide.

concubine: A young male slave used for sexual release until his master marries.

condone: To accept (behaviour that is considered morally wrong or offensive).

consensual: Relating to or involving consent or consensus.

conspire: To make secret plans jointly to commit an unlawful or harmful act.

constitution: A body of fundamental principles or established precedents according to which a state or other organization is acknowledged to be governed: 'Britain lacks a codified constitution'

contention: Something that is argued.

conviction: The quality of showing that one is firmly convinced of what one believes or says.

cordial: To be warm or friendly.

culture: The ideas, customs, and social behaviour of a particular people or society.

decisive: Having or showing the ability to make decisions quickly and effectively.

defamatory: (of remarks, writing, etc.) Damaging the good reputation of someone; slanderous or libellous.

democracy: A system of government by the whole population or all the eligible members of a state, typically through elected representatives.

deposition: To oust someone out of power.

dialectical: Relating to the logical discussion of ideas and opinions.

disciplines: Relating to modules or studies.

dissident: A person who opposes official policy, especially that of an authoritarian state.

docile: To be ready to accept control or instruction; submissive.

economic inequality: The disparity in wealth, distribution and opportunities among people belonging to different groups, communities, or countries.

empowerment: The process of becoming stronger and more confident, especially in controlling one's life and claiming one's rights.

equality: The state of being equal, especially in status, rights, or opportunities.

exonerate: (of an official body) T%o absolve (someone) from blame for a fault or wrongdoing.

extortion: The practice of obtaining something, especially money, through force or threats.

fallacy: A mistaken belief, especially one based on unsound arguments.

feminism: The advocacy of women's rights based on the equality of the sexes.

frivolous: Not having any serious purpose or value.

fruitful: To produce good or helpful results; productive.

gender: The attitudes, behaviours, norms, and roles that a society or culture associates with an individual's sex, thus the social differences between female and male; the meanings attached to being feminine or masculine.

gender parity: The situation when each gender is represented equally.

giggle: To laugh lightly and repeatedly in a silly way, from amusement, nervousness, or embarrassment.

hormonal: To be affected by one's sex hormones, especially to feel moody or easily aroused.

idiosyncrasy: A mode of behaviour or way of thought peculiar to an individual.

indoctrinate: To teach (a person or group) to accept a set of beliefs uncritically.

judiciary: The judicial authorities of a country; judges collectively.

justice: The quality of being fair and reasonable.
lavish: To be sumptuously rich, elaborate, or luxurious.

LGBTQI: Relating to homosexual; lesbian, gay, bisexual, transgender, queer, and intersex.

masquerade: An action or appearance that is mere disguise or show.

misogyny: A dislike of, contempt for, or ingrained prejudice against women.

monstrous: To be inhumanly or outrageously evil or wrong.

norms: The standards of proper or acceptable behaviour.

noteworthy: To be worth paying attention to; interesting or significant.

NPO: Non-profit organisation.

oppress: To keep (someone) in subjection and hardship, especially by the unjust exercise of authority.

painstaking: Done with or employing great care and thoroughness.

perplexed: Unable to understand something clearly or to think clearly.

pathophysiology: The disordered physiological processes associated with disease or injury.

polygamous: Relating to or involving polygamy; the practice or custom of having more than one wife at the same time.

polyandry: A form of polygamy in which a woman takes two or more husbands at the same time.

powers and privileges: Power is the ability to influence and make decisions that impact others. Privilege refers to the advantages and benefits that individuals receive because of the social groups they are perceived to be a part of. Privilege is often a result of systematic targeting and/or marginalisation of another social group.

promiscuous: Having or characterized by many transient sexual relationships.

prosecute: To institute or conduct legal proceedings against (a person or organisation).

puzzled: Unable to understand; perplexed.

psychiatry: The branch of medicine concerned with the study, diagnosis, and treatment of mental illness.

quarrelsome: The state of being argumentative or confrontational.

ratification: The act of making something officially valid by signing it or otherwise giving it formal consent.

reckless: Heedless of danger or the consequences of one's actions; rash or impetuous.

recommendation: A suggestion or proposal as to the best course of action, especially one put forward by an authoritative body.

redeem: compensate for the faults or bad aspects of.

resolution: A firm decision to do or not to do something.

retrieve: To get or bring (something) back from somewhere.

rhetoric: The art of effective or persuasive speaking or writing, especially the exploitation of figures of speech and other compositional techniques.

rights: That which is morally correct, just, or honourable.

Rule of Law: The restriction of the arbitrary exercise of power by subordinating it to well-defined and established laws.

selfish: (of a person, action, or motive) Lacking consideration for other people; concerned chiefly with one's profit or pleasure.

sentiments: The views or opinions that are held or expressed.

sex: Either of the two main categories (male and female) into which humans and most other living things are divided based on their reproductive functions.

sexual orientation: This refers to who individuals feel attracted to, while gender identity refers to one's self-concept of being male, female, or non-binary.

short-sighted: To be lacking imagination or foresight.

spiteful: To show or be caused by malice.

social construction: Things that are generally viewed as natural or normal in society, such as understandings of gender, race, class, and disability, are socially constructed, and consequently aren't an accurate reflection of reality.

socialisation: The action or process of making something socialistic, or a behaviour that is socially accepted. Relating to teaching.

solidarity: A unity or agreement of feeling or action, especially among individuals with a common interest; mutual support within a group.

soothe: To gently calm (a person or their feelings).

stakeholder: Someone who has a direct or indirect interest in the company's operations, activities, or consequences, such as a person, group, organisation, government, or other institution. They can be internal (primary) or external (secondary), depending on their association with the company that serves their interests.

stern: (of a person or their manner) Serious and unrelenting, especially in the assertion of authority and exercise of discipline.

supress: To prevent the development, action, or expression of (a feeling, impulse, idea, etc.); restrain.

testosterone: The primary sex hormone and anabolic steroid in males. In humans, testosterone plays a key role in the development of male reproductive tissues such as the testes and prostate, as well as promoting secondary sexual characteristics such as increased muscle and bone mass, and the growth of body hair.

toxic: To be poisonous; something that is poisonous.

UN Charter: The constitutive instrument of the United Nations, signed on 26 June 1945. It sets out the rights and obligations of member states and establishes the principal organs and procedures of the United Nations.

unravel: To undo undo (twisted, knitted, or woven threads).

Untermensch: A Nazi term for non-Aryan people they deem as inferior, who were often referred to as 'the masses from the East'.

uppity: To be above oneself, self-important; arrogant, snobbish, haughty.

values: Socially approved desires and goals that are internalised through the process of conditioning, learning or socialisation and that become subjective preferences, standards, and aspirations.

vilify: To speak or write about in an abusively disparaging manner.

3. The vernacular vocabulary you need to understand to fully grasp the main and minor plots of Poison (vernacular)

Indoda eshaywa umfazi: A sentence derived from the Zulu language. '*Indoda*' is a man in English. '*Eshaywa*' means to beat and '*umfazi*' is a woman. So, in a nutshell, '*indoda eshaywa umfazi*' means, 'a man who is being beaten by a woman'.

Isfebe: A derogatory Zulu word that refers to a woman who cheats or a prostitute.

Isoka: A Zulu word that refers to a boyfriend, especially one who has a lot of girlfriends at the same time.

Malibongwe igama lamakhosikazi: A popular Zulu slogan that arose during the apartheid era in South Africa. During that era, women played a vital role in the struggle against apartheid, especially women who were wives to the struggle activists (men). For example, when Nelson Mandela was in prison, Winnie Mandela took care of the Mandela family and their children. In addition, Winnie Mandela continued with the legacy of Nelson Mandela. In other words, women filled a political void that was left by men (struggle activists); who were either exiled or imprisoned. Another popular example was in 1956 when women marched to the Union Buildings (South African Presidential Offices) to protest against the apartheid laws. This march was led by women, namely Helen Joseph, Rahima Moosa, Sophia Williams-De Bruyn and Lillian Ngoyi. The phrase '*Malibongwe igama LaMakhosikazi*' arose during this time and it translates as: '*Let us praise women, we appreciate women* or *we are grateful for women.*'

Malume: An Nguni (Zulu, Ndebele, Swati and Xhosa) word which refers to an *uncle* in English.

Mama, ndiwufumen' umsebenzi: A typical Xhosa phrase. '*Mama*' means mother; not only in Xhosa but in Nguni languages. '*Ndiwufumene*' means 'I got'. '*Umsebenzi*' means 'a job'. Therefore, this sentence translates as follows: 'Mother, I got a job.'

Sanibonani: An Nguni word for greeting. '*Sanibonani*' means; 'hello', and 'good day' (good morning, good afternoon and good evening).

Wathinta abafazi wathina imbokodo: This Zulu phrase originated after the 1956 Women's March to the Union Buildings. As I stated, women played a vital role in advancing the struggle against apartheid. '*Wathinta*' means to touch, '*abafazi*' refers to women, '*imbokodo*' refers to a rock. Therefore, this phrase translates as: '*If you strike a woman, you strike a rock.*'

4. The structural elements of a plot

Exposition

Exposition refers to the portion of a story/play that introduces important background information to the audience. This includes the setting, events occurring before the main plot, characters and any backstories.

The exposition of *Poison* is seen through the introductory dialogues of its five characters. Noteworthy is that these successive introductions introduce background events and characters.

Rising action

Rising action pertains to the events or series of conflicts in a play that lead to and culminate in a climax.

The first inciting incident in *Poison* is brought on by Nelson. This inciting incident comes after Edward has stipulated the rules of the table. Nelson asks a controversial question and then proceeds to make controversial remarks.

Why are we having this committee to begin with? When we advocate for gender parity and women empowerment, it seems like we do it at the expense of vilifying men. In fact, chairman, I am convinced that this Briefing Committee is nothing but a weapon formed against men!

This marks the rising action of *Poison*.

Climax

The **climax** is the most intense or exciting part of the story.

The climax unfolds when the war of words ensues. In this case, I use ad hominem (undermining the character's credibility/attack on ethcs) to intensify the climax of *Poison*. The exchange of tarnishing words happens between Buhlebendalo and Itumeleng; thus, demarcating the climax of *Poison*.

ITUMELENG

My fellow committee members, allow me to say this. I think Buhlebendalo belongs to that toxic brigade that you have been talking about, the feminists. She is one of those women who disrespect men. She is part of that agenda.

BUHLEBENDALO

Don't you dare label and disrespect me. Don't you dare!

If that is the case, you Itumeleng belong to that branch of fragile women who cannot stand up for themselves .

Nonetheless, the highest point of the story unfolds when Itumeleng exclaims the word 'enough' three times. Thus, marking the second scene of *Poison*. In this scene, Itumeleng begins her soliloquy. The soliloquy is emotional and sets a precedence for an intense atmosphere.'

Falling action

Falling action refers to **when** the conflict in a drama begins to be resolved.

The falling action of *Poison* unfolds during the Itumeleng's lengthy soliloquy. In this scene, we observe a paradigm shift.

Itumeleng diverges from her initial line of thought. Initially, she maintained that women ought to be humble and remain still even in the most unbearable circumstances. However, after her soliloquy, Itumeleng encourages women to stand up for themselves.

Resolution

The element of resolution, also known as denouement or conclusion is the final part of a play where a resolution or conclusion is reached.

In the resolution of *Poison,* interesting events unfold. Firstly, catharses are seen through the characters of Itumeleng and Nelson. The catharsis of Itumeleng' is seen through her emotional soliloquy. The catharsis of Nelson' is seen when he begins to sob.

(At this point, ITUMELENG goes back to her chair. She sits next to a teary and emotional NELSON. Seemingly, his emotions are overwhelming him. Apparently, he is drowning in a pool of pain and sorrow.

(He can't help but give ITUMELENG a tight hug. He begins to sob over her shoulder and together they begin to sob.)

At this point, it seems like all characters are sympathetic to the cause of the feminists and the plight of women in general. Buhlebendalo, as the protagonist, makes her final soliloquy. She affirms her line of thought and rhetoric unopposed.

This marks the denouement of *Poison*.

5. Style, diction, syntax and figures of speech

Alliteration

Alliteration is the repetition of consonant sounds, particularly at the start of sentences. An example of alliteration from the play is: *'Good as Gold'*

Allusion

Allusion refers to another artistic work, person, place or idea well known to the audience to use its meaning or characteristics to illustrate the author's message.

These are two examples of allusion from *Poison*:

Can you ever imagine a situation where it would be said; 'a woman who once had 700 husbands and 300 concubines?'

And

I for one will rather choose a foolish virgin than marry a Mary Magdalene.

In fact, give me all ten virgins; the foolish and the wise!

Anaphora

Anaphora is a form of parallelism. It refers to the repetition of words at the beginning of successive clauses in a sentence. This helps to add emphasis and build momentum.

This is an example of anaphora from *Poison*:

It was Eve who gave Adam the apple; it was Alexandra who poisoned Alexandrovich's mind; it was Marie who poisoned Louis' mind; it was Grace who poisoned Mugabe's mind; and it was Delilah who cut Samson's hair and compromised him.

This is another example:

Because of false accusations of rape, many have lost their livelihoods.

Many have lost their jobs.

Many have lost their erstwhile friends.

Many have been subjected to the torment of social exclusion.

Many have been maltreated by their family members.

Antithesis

Antithesis refers to a pair of opposing terms, clauses or phrases that are in direct juxtaposition. This happens effectively in contradictions and contraries. It happens in a setting of parallelism, which works well to emphasise the opposition of terms, clauses or phrases.

In the play antithesis is seen in Itumeleng's words: '*a man must be a man and a woman must be a woman.*'

Ad hominem

Ad hominem is a personal attack on a speaker, usually to undermine the credibility of that person.

These are examples of the use of ad hominem(s) from *Poison*:

ITUMELENG

My fellow committee members, allow me to say this. I think Buhlebendalo belongs to that toxic brigade that you have been talking about, the feminists. She is one of those women who disrespect men. She is part of that agenda.

BUHLEBENDALO

Don't you dare label and disrespect me. Don't you dare!

If that is the case, you Itumeleng belong to that branch of fragile women who cannot stand up for themselves

Ad populum

Ad populum refers to a well-known phenomenon, person, or historical aspect or uses emotions to appeal to an audience.

In *Poison*, we see this element in the usage of the parable of ten virgins from the Bible and also the reference to the story of Samson.

Assonance

Assonance refers to the repetition of vowel sounds.

In *Poison*, assonance is evident in the extract: *'where men cheat and expect to be forgiven'.* In this example, the key vowel sound is seen through the repetition of the letter 'e'.

Cause and effect

The element of cause and effect must show that a certain outcome is a result of a particular action.

Chiasmus

Chiasmus refers **to** a two-part sentence or phrase; where the second phrase is the reversal of the first part.

An example from *Poison* is 'A man must not be a woman and a woman must not be a man.'

Leading or complex question

A leading or complex question is a question posed to prompt the respondent or the witness to answer in a specific manner, or as desired by the advocate.

These are two examples from *Poison*:

Could Kwame Nkrumah be correct when he argues in the first chapter of his book Ghana that 'Women by nature are quarrelsome and men by nature are polygamous'?

And,

If I am getting you correctly, according to your books, feminists are a 'bunch' of poisonous women who have something to do with lying. Correct?

Modes of appeal: Logos, ethos and pathos

Logos appeals to the audience's reason, building up logical arguments.

This is an example from *Poison*:

My fellow committee members, our constitution must protect us like an eagle protecting its nest. We are all under the wings of law, therefore, there must be justice for everyone who has been wronged in any way.

In the case of false accusation of rape and exoneration, if the falsely accused requires a formal apology from the accuser. Perhaps for forgiveness and finding closure (waving her hands) it then becomes the responsibility of the accuser to issue out such an apology.

This is another example from the play:

To understand a certain problem comprehensively. One has to understand its roots – what we call the root of a problem. Once we understand the root of a problem, not only will we be able to understand the problem, but we will also be able to come up with solutions for that problem and prevent it from repeating itself.

Ethos appeals to the speaker's credibility, making the audience more likely to trust him or her.

The introductions of all characters of *Poison* where they speak about their representative stakeholders, the offices they lead, for example, a chairperson, and the qualifications they have is a good example of ethos.

In the play, the following words of Buhlebendalo serve as an apt example of ethos:

I have studied many literatures from different parts of the world in my lifetime. Particularly literature on gender equality and gender parity.

Pathos appeals to the emotions in an attempt to make the audience angry or sympathetic.

Buhlebendalo's words, seen in the following extract from the play serve as a good example of this element:

Throughout the ages of time, history recognises or justifies the actions of men at the expense of either vilifying women or portraying them as nonentities, conspirators, servants and aides.

Parallelism

Parallelism relates to a pair of phrases, words, sentences or clauses with the same grammatical structure.

The following extract from the play (dialogue by Nelson) is a fine example of the use of parallelism:

We want them to be Alpha males.

We want them to grow manes and be kings.

We want them to be top dogs in life.

We want them to win in every battle of life.

We want them to be top achievers in their courses.

We want them to excel in fashion and gentlemanliness.

And we want them to become beasts in sports.

This is another example of parallelism in *Poison* (spoken by Buhlebendalo):

In the domain of religion, we want to see women leading as pastors and priests, not as ushers and servants.

In the domain of politics, we want to see women leading as presidents and ministers, not as personal assistants and secretaries for presidents and ministers.

Polyptoton

Polyptoton is the stylistic scheme in which words derived from the same root are repeated.

This is an example of polyptoton in *Poison*: *'Sadly, what is done cannot be undone.'*

Another example is: *'Using dangerous words in general is dangerous.'*

Rhyme

Rhyme is the correspondence of sound between words or the endings of words.

One example from *Poison* is: 'women have always been oppressed and suppressed.'

Another example is: 'single as a pringle.'

Similarity

The element of similarity means that examples that are made in an inductive argument must be analogous.

This is an example from the dialogue in the play (spoken by Buhlebendalo):

Before the Russian Revolution, Alexandra Feodorovna suffered the calamity of being constantly accused of conspiring with Grigori Rasputin against her husband Nikolai Alexandrovich Romanov.

Before the French Revolution, Marie Antoinette suffered the calamity of being disparaged as a 'frivolous, selfish, and immoral woman whose lavish lifestyle had increased economic inequality.'

Before Robert Mugabe's deposition, Grace Mugabe was always perceived as a 'whispering serpent' to Robert Mugabe's ears.

Testimony

The topic of testimony in an inductive logic makes use of examples.

This extract from the play (spoken by Buhlebendalo) is a good example of testimony:

The word 'Untermensch' resulted in a genocide of more than six million people in Nazi Germany.

The word 'dissidents' resulted in a genocide of more than 20 thousand people in Zimbabwe.

The word 'cockroaches' resulted in a genocide of more than 800 thousand people in Rwanda.

www.ingramcontent.com/pod-product-compliance
Lightning Source LLC
LaVergne TN
LVHW052044160826
845678LV00015B/3112

* 9 7 8 1 7 7 6 4 2 5 6 0 0 *